**RECORD SNOWFALL IN THE NORTH ATLANTIC STATES CAUSE[ ]
80 DEATHS. NEW YORK CITY SUFFERED 25.8" OF SNOW.**

It was the year the **Cold War** heated up, with anticommunism looming large in America's mind. The president issued the Truman Doctrine, stating the principle of Soviet containment. Russia respond-ed by attacking the U.S. in the UN for war-mongering.

The National Security Act unified all branch[ ] of the armed service into a single branch, t[ ] new Department of Defense.

Secretary of State Marshall proposed the European Recovery Program, better known as the Marshall Plan, to give economic aid to war-torn European nation[ ]

The federal government was attacked for loose security, and President Truman initiated a loyalty program for civil servants.

FLASH!

The Supreme Court upheld state law permitting parochial school pupils to ride on state-funded buses.

newsreel

The wartime draft was brought to an end. Two days before Christmas, Truman granted pardons to 1,523 who were convicted of evading the World War II draft.

Congress enacted the Taft-Hartley Act over the president's veto. The law limited the power of labor unions, including restrictions on strikes and political activities.

On May 29, when a Cleveland-bound United Airlines plane crashed minutes after takeoff at La Guardia Airport in New York City, 42 people were burned to death, making it the worst accident in the history of commercial aviation.

3

Faced with a far-ranging crisis, **England** nationalized coal mines, cable and radio communications, and the electrical supply industry.

British India was divided into the independent states of India (Hindu) and Pakistan (Muslim).

Communist parties in Europe established Cominform, the **Communist Information Bureau**.

headlines

international

ON NOVEMBER 29, THE U.N. VOTED TO PARTITION PALESTINE INTO TWO SECTORS, ONE JEWISH AND ONE ARAB.

In Nicaragua, **General Anastasio Somoza**, president for more than 10 years, overthrew his successor, the democratically elected Leonardo Arguello, after Arguello had been in office 26 days.

4

On July 18, 4,554 Jews on board the *Exodus 1947* were denied access to Palestine when Britain refused to let them disembark at the port of Haifa. On September 7, the "souls without a country" were forced to return to Germany, where they were sent to an internment camp.

Monster typhoons and flooding killed 1,692 people on Honshu Island, Japan.

Communists gained control of Manchuria in the Chinese civil war with the Nationalists.

Remains of the first **dinosaurs** inhabiting America 200 million year
earlier were discovered near Albuquerque by a team from New York
American Museum of Natural History.

Congressman Richard Nixon and the House Committee to Investigate Un-American Activities held hearings on Communists in the movie business. Actors Ronald Reagan and Robert Taylor, among others, participated in the Red hunt. Anti-HUAC actors included Humphrey Bogart, Gene Kelly, and Lauren Bacall, who flew to Washington, DC, to protest the hearings. On November 25, the Motion Picture Association named 10 "subversives"—the Hollywood 10—who were banned from work in the industry. Among these were director Edward Dmytryk *(Farewell My Lovely)*, and screenwriter Ring Lardner, Jr. *(Woman of the Year)*.

Young **Marlon Brando** shocked audiences as the brutal, T-shirt-wearing Stanley Kowalski in Tennessee Williams's *A Streetcar Named Desire.*

'47
cultural
milestones

A COPY OF THE FIRST EDITION OF THE *BAY PSALM BOOK* WAS SOLD IN NEW YORK FOR $115,000, THE HIGHEST PRICE EVER PAID FOR A BOOK.

1,000 NEW JOKES

FRED ALLEN

radio

Champion of Champions **Fred Allen, Bing Crosby, Lux Radio Theatre**

Star of Tomorrow **Jack Paar, Abe Burrows, Robert Q. Lewis**

Comedian **Fred Allen, Henry Morgan, Bob Hope**

Comedienne **Joan Davis, Gracie Allen, Fannie Brice**

Comedy Team **Fibber McGee and Molly, Burns and Allen, Abbott and Costello**

Master of Ceremonies **Bing Crosby, Ralph Edwards, Arthur Godfrey**

Film Personality Most Effective on Radio **Bing Crosby, Bob Hope, Ronald Colman**

Male Vocalist: Popular–**Bing Crosby, Perry Como, Frank Sinatra**

Female Vocalist: Popular–**Dinah Shore, Jo Stafford, Ginny Sims, Peggy Lee**

Sportscaster **Bill Stern, Red Barber, Mel Allen**

S premiered "Strike It Rich,"
he quiz show with a heart."

ch week, a batch of poor unfor-
mates would plead for help,
d the studio audience decided
nich wretch got the loot.

television

t the beginning
f the year, there
vere an estimated
0,000 TV sets
n use. By year's
nd, the number
pproached
57,000.

On May 7, NBC put "Kraft Television Theater" on the air, testing TV's power as an advertising medium. For 2 weeks, all ads on the show were for Imperial Cheese. While perky model Dana Wyatt demonstrated "tastability," announcer Ed Herlihy talked up this miracle of dairy technology. By week 3, every package of Imperial Cheese in New York City was bought off the shelves.

9

science

On October 14, **Chuck Yeager** became the first human being to travel faster than the speed of sound. He piloted his Bell X-1 rocket plane, Glamorous Glennis, to Mach 1.06, or 750 mph, breaking the sound barrier.

In archaeology, a Bedouin shepherd boy in Wadi Qumran discovered a cave containing the **Dead Sea Scrolls**, which included a record of the Essenes, a monastic cult, and a copy of the Old Testament dating back to the 1st century B.C.

American aviator William Odom completed flight around the globe on August 10. Odom made his orbit in record-breaking 73 hours, 5 minutes and 11 seconds, more than 18 hours faster than the 1938 record set by Howard Hughes.

celeb wedding

Princess Elizabeth, daughter of King George VI and Queen Elizabeth, married her cousin, **Prince Philip**, Duke of Edinburgh, before a crowd of notables at Westminster Abbey. As the triumphal procession made its way to Buckingham Palace, thousands of Londoners cheered them along.

10

celeb births

DAVID BOWIE, androgynous rock star, in England, on January 8.

FARRAH FAWCETT, Charlie's Angel and popular big-haired poster woman, in Corpus Christi, TX, on February 2.

EDWARD JAMES OLMOS, film actor, in Boyle Heights, CA, on February 24.

BILLY CRYSTAL, actor, comedian, and Oscars host, March 14, in Long Beach, NY.

GLENN CLOSE, actress, on March 19, in Greenwich, CT.

ELTON JOHN, singer and piano player, March 25 in Middlesex, England.

EMMYLOU HARRIS, country singer-songwriter, in Birmingham, AL, on April 2.

DAVID LETTERMAN, late-night talk show host, in Indianapolis, IN, on April 12.

JAMES WOODS, actor, in Vernal, UT, April 18.

DOUG HENNING, magician, in Ft. Gary, Manitoba, May 3.

SALMAN RUSHDIE, fugitive author of *The Satanic Verses*, in Bombay, India, on June 19.

O. J. SIMPSON, retired football great, actor and celebrity homicide defendant, was born on July 9.

CARLOS SANTANA, guitarist, in Mexico, July 20.

ALBERT BROOKS, actor-comedian-writer, born Albert Laurence Einstein in Beverly Hills, CA, on July 22.

DON HENLEY, musician, member of the Eagles, July 22, in Gilmer, TX.

ARNOLD SCHWARZENEGGER, movie star and bodybuilder, July 30, in Graz, Austria.

KEVIN KLINE, actor, St. Louis, MO, on October 24.

PAT SAJAK, "Wheel of Fortune" host, October 26, Chicago.

RICHARD DREYFUSS, movie star, Brooklyn, October 29.

JOHN LARROQUETTE, TV sitcom star, New Orleans, November 25.

TED DANSON, "Cheers" star and film actor, December 29, in San Diego, CA.

DEATHS

Ogden Mills Reid, publisher of the influential *New York Herald Tribune*, died on January 3.

Pierre Bonnard, French painter, 79 years old, died on January 23.

Al Capone, gangster, longtime leader of the Chicago mob, died of apoplexy on January 25.

Grace Moore, 45-year-old American opera singer and film star, and Prince Gustaf Adolf, eldest son of the Crown Prince of Sweden, were killed on January 26 when their KLM Dutch airplane crashed in Copenhagen.

Carrie Chapman Catt, famous American woman's suffrage activist, died on March 9. She was 88.

Henry Ford, 83-year-old founder of Ford Motor Company and the father of mass production, died on April 7.

Willa Cather, novelist, author of *Death Comes for the Archbishop* and the Pulitzer Prize-winning *One of Ours*, died on April 24.

Maxwell Perkins, the editor who helped shape the careers of Thomas Wolfe, F. Scott Fitzgerald, and Ernest Hemingway, died on June 17.

Fiorello La Guardia, colorful ex-mayor of New York City, died on September 20.

milestones

MILLION SELLING RECORDS

i'll hold you in my heart
(Victor), Eddy Arnold & His Texas Plowboys

here comes santa claus
(Columbia), Gene Autry

when you were sweet sixteen
(Victor), Perry Como, with The Satisfiers and
Lloyd Schaffer's Orchestra

near you
(Bullet), Francis Craig and His Orchestra

open the door, richard!
(National), Dusty Fletcher

move on up a little higher
(Apollo), Mahalia Jackson

too fat polka
(Columbia), Arthur Godfrey

hit music

'47

Dusty Fletcher's "Open the Door, Richard!" became the nuisance song of the year. The novelty hit, from a well-known vaudeville routine in Black theater, was recorded by Jack McVea, Count Basie, Louis Jordan, and the Three Flames.

Most popular female singers of the year were **Jo Stafford** and **Dinah Shore**. Most popular male crooners were **Perry Como**, **Buddy Clark**, and **Art Lund**. Favorite bands were those conducted by **Ted Weems**, **Eddy Howard**, and **Francis Craig**. The combos of choice were the **Harmonicats**, the **Three Suns**, and the **King Cole Trio**. Fueled by "Zip-A-Dee-Doo-Dah," from Disney's *Song of the South*, a barnful of doggedly rural tunes drove the country wild. "Feudin' and Fightin'," "Huggin' and Chalkin'," and "A Gal in Calico" led this hillbilly hit parade.

fiction

1. **gentleman's agreement**
   by laura z. hobson

2. **prince of foxes**
   by samuel shellabarger

3. **kingsblood royal**
   by sinclair lewis

4. **the moneyman**
   by thomas b. costain

5. **lydia bailey**
   by kenneth roberts

6. **the wayward bus**
   by john steinbeck

7. **the miracle of the bells**
   by russell janney

8. **the vixens**
   by frank yerby

9. **house divided**
   by ben ames williams

10. **east side, west side**
    by marcia davenport

Tales of the South Pacific, published this year by James A. Michener, became the basis for the Broadway show and movie *South Pacific*. Now a U.S. citizen, Thomas Mann published *Doctor Faustus*, an allegorical novel about the rise of Nazism. *Anne Frank: The Diary of a Young Girl*, written by Anne Frank while living in hiding during the Nazi persecution of the Jews in the Netherlands, was published by her father this year. 78-year-old Frenchman André Gide won the Nobel Prize for Literature. Robert Penn Warren won the Pulitzer Prize for *All the King's Men*. Robert Lowell won the Pulitzer Prize in poetry for *Lord Weary's Castle*. *I, The Jury*, Mickey Spillane's tough-guy masterpiece, hit the stands this year. Malcolm Lowry published his famous drunk-alogue *Under the Volcano*.

Two of this year's top sellers, *Gentleman's Agreement* and *Kingsblood Royal*, dealt with interfaith and interracial relations, respectively.

books

nonfiction

Despite 7 hits by Brooklyn Dodger Jackie Robinson, the Yankees took their 11th World Series. Joe DiMaggio, Phil Rizzuto and Yogi Berra helped the Bronx Bombers win the 7th game, 5–2.

Jackie Robinson, the first Black baseball player in the major leagues, started the season at first base for the Brooklyn Dodgers.

In tennis, Jack Kramer, 2-time winner of the U.S. Open, became the first American to win Wimbledon since Bobby Riggs in 1939.

In boxing, champion **Joe Louis** racked up another victory, this one on points, over Jersey Joe Walcott.

In the annual military matchup, Navy routed its Army rival, 21–0.

sports'47

In Pasadena, Illinois trounced UCLA, 45–14, in the Rose Bowl on New Year's Day.

French racer Jean Robic won the first Tour de France held since the war.

In Scotland, Mildred "Babe" Didrikson Zaharias became the first American to win the British Open golf title.

WELCOME STRANGE.

oscar winners

Best Picture **Gentleman's Agreement**

Best Actor **Ronald Colman,**
A Double Life

Best Actress **Loretta Young,**
The Farmer's Daughter

Best Supporting Actor
Edmund Gwenn, *Miracle on 34th Street*

Best Supporting Actress
Celeste Holm, *Gentleman's Agreement*

Best Director **Elia Kazan,**
Gentleman's Agreement

Best Original Screenplay
The Bachelor and the Bobby-Soxer,
by Sidney Sheldon

Best Adapted Screenplay
Miracle on 34th Street,
by George Seaton

hit movies

1. *Welcome Stranger*
   Paramount $6,100,000

2. *The Egg and I*
   Universal-International $5,500,000

3. *Unconquered*
   Paramount $5,250,000

4. *Life With Father*
   Warner Bros. $5,057,000

5. *Forever Amber*
   20th Century-Fox $5,000,000

TOP 10 BOX-OFFICE STARS
1. Bing Crosby
2. Betty Grable
3. Van Johnson
4. Gary Cooper
5. Abbott and Costello
6. Ingrid Bergman
7. Bob Hope
8. Humphrey Bogart
9. Spencer Tracy
10. Cary Grant

movies

Forever Amber, though one of the biggest hits of the season, actually lost money for 20th Century-Fox. The Catholic Legion of Decency asked that all of the love scenes be cut; director Otto Preminger refused. After this, the film was banned, labeled by the Church "a glorification of immorality and licentiousness."

THE EGG AND I

cars

The popularity of "Drive now, pay later" plans among American car buyers swelled the amount of installment credit outstanding for new cars from $544 million in 1946 to more than $1 billion by the end of 1947.

The Tucker Corporation's "48" pilot model was unveiled this summer in Chicago. The Tucker Torpedo featured a rear engine and a 3rd headlamp that turned with the front wheels.

otor vehicle owners paid out more xes in 1947 for the purchase and eration of their new vehicles than any previous year in U.S. history.

The Mack Truck, LR Off-Highway Model, earned the nickname Packhorse of Heavy Construction for its constant use in postwar rebuilding.

Christian Dior burst onto the scene this year with his ultrafeminine collection. Dior's corsets, high pumps, sleek gloves, cocktail hats, and umbrellas all caught fashion-conscious America's imagination. His silhouette, with its long skirts, nipped-in waist, and sloping shoulders, was heralded as a watershed—the final death knell for wartime fashions. One by-product of the Dior Look: the petticoats, padding, and built-in corsetry made them very, very heavy.

fashion

With the new sloping shoulder line, neckline became a focus of interest, with Bonaparte roll collars, stand-away, face-framing, and collarless neck lines all being seen. Some American designer favored the short bolero or bell-hop suit jacke Many women favored jackets that padded over th hips and were fitted—to emphasize a tiny waist.

'47

22

On January 28, the borough of Manhattan retired its **last trolley car** in a sentimental ceremony. The fleet was replaced by diesel buses.

final factoid

credits

archive photos: inside front cover, pages 1, 3, 6, 10, 15, 20, 24, inside back cover.

associated press: pages 2, 4, 5, 10, 16, 17, 23

photofest: pages 7, 8, 13, 18, 19

photo research:
alice albert

coordination:
rustyn birch

design:
carol bokuniewicz design
paul ritter

'47